Science of Parenthood's

The Big Book of
Parenting
Tweets

Featuring the
most hilarious
parents on Twitter

Kate Hall and Science of Parenthood

SCIENCE OF PARENTHOOD PRESS

ISBN-13: 978-1503189553

ISBN-10: 1503189554

Edited by Kate Hall, Norine Dworkin-McDaniel and Jessica Ziegler

Design and Cover by Jessica Ziegler

Science of Parenthood books are available at a special discount when purchased in bulk for premiums and sale promotion as well as for fundraising or educational use. Special editions or book excerpts also can be created to specification.

For details, contact info@scienceofparenthood.com.

Science of Parenthood Press
342 Lake Amberleigh Dr. Winter Garden Fl 34787
scienceofparenthood.com

SCIENCE OF PARENTHOOD is a registered trademark of Science of Parenthood, LLC.

Printed in the United States of America
First printing November 2014

Dedicated to the 85 children
who provide us with so much material.

So very, very much material.

Contents

Preface | vii

Introduction | xiii

Part 1: WAKE UP! It's GO Time! | 19

Part 2: Afternoon Delight? Yeah, Right. | 65

Part 3: The Bitching Hours | 113

Glossary | 167

Contributors | 177

Acknowledgments | 189

About the Editors | 193

Preface

by Kate Hall

Why would anyone want to squeeze their thoughts and ideas into 140 characters or less and share them on the Internet? What *is* the point?

That's what I wondered when a friend encouraged me to join Twitter to promote my blog back in 2012. At first I felt like I was standing alone on the moon, shouting into the seemingly empty Twitterverse around me. Occasionally one of my tweets would get a star (Twitter for "favoriting"), or the highly coveted retweet (or share) was thrown my way. Those rare virtual high-fives were enough to keep me going.

Then I came across a joke on Twitter: a one-liner. Then I found more. I discovered an entire subculture of Twitter comedians! There were thousands of "tweeps" sharing their wit and snark in 140 characters or less. And they were *funny*. It was like being at a comedy club while lying in bed, unshowered, eating a candy bar. I began closely following my favorite funny tweeps, not wanting to miss a single joke.

One night, I retweeted a joke that made me laugh. That tweep noticed, then starred and retweeted about ten of my tweets. That was exciting. Still, I was nervous about putting my jokes out there with all these talented people. I feared my quips would fall—thud —like a wet swim diaper after a day at the pool.

But my quip got a star. And then a retweet. Then more stars! And more retweets! Oh, the validation! I was hooked! I spent more time on Twitter, writing and reading, starring and retweeting. I read books on how to write comedy to make my tweets even better. I became slightly obsessed.

A year and a half later, I've read more than 100,000 tweets. Each month, I publish the best I've read in a Top 10 Funniest Tweets List on my blog, Hall of Tweets (HallOf Tweets.com). Along the way, I've gotten to know many of these Twitter comedians personally, not only through their tweets but also through interviews I've done with them for my site. For the most part, these comics aren't professional stand-ups or TV joke writers. Many of them work as teachers, doctors, marketing managers or stay-at-home moms and dads, slogging through the same bedtime routines, dinner snafus and bathroom misses we all are.

Weirdly though, Twitter has made me a better parent. A better mom. These days, I find that I don't get as upset when my kids spill milk or raid my hidden candy stash. Instead, I think, "I'll tweet about that." The humor I read every day on Twitter has helped change my perspective and has made me feel less alone—like I'm not the only parent who feels clueless or thinks my kids are being little jerks sometimes.

In these pages, Jessica, Norine and I have collected our favorite tweets from the tweeps who have us rolling at our own parenting mishaps. Many of them routinely make my Funniest Tweets List and snare coveted spots on *The Huffington Post*'s weekly Funniest Tweets from Parents lists. Check them out, laugh out loud, then go follow the contributors on Twitter and prepare to laugh some more.

Introduction

"I don't get Twitter."

Unless you work in social media, asking
people if they are on Twitter will often result
in one of the following responses:

Twitter is for breaking news and stuff, right?
I get my news from Facebook, thanks.
Twitter is too hard.
Why are you asking me about birds?

Twitter can be daunting to the uninitiated. The first-time foray is like jumping right into river rapids. One-hundred-and-forty-character missives go rushing by, peppered with indecipherable abbreviations and acronyms: DM, RT, FF, TC.

#OMG what is HAPPENING here?

It is all a bit much. But if you spend some time immersed in the stream, you will begin to figure it out, and find the people (or "tweeps") who are sharing compelling content, or better yet, hilarious jokes. Mini-morsels of wit. Perfect nuggets of comedy gold.

Ah, but to find the time to dig for that gold! No one has it—least of all over-worked, under-showered, sleep-deprived parents. That's why we've done all the hard work for you.

Science of Parenthood has teamed up with Twitter all-star Kate Hall of Hall of Tweets to put together *The Big Book of Parenting Tweets*, a collection of more than 300 of the most hysterical tweets from the funniest Twitter comedians who also happen to be parents just like you.

So, whether you are grabbing three uninterrupted minutes in the bathroom—ha!—or thirty seconds before your toddler's next meltdown, 140 characters* are the perfect length for a busy parent's over-taxed attention span. Don't worry, as the kids get older, your attention span will increase. Why, before you know it, you'll be reading for *ten minutes at a stretch!* Until then, have some tweets. We bet you can't read just one.

If you are Twitter stickler—a Twickler, if you will —you may notice that some of these tweets go over 140 characters. Editorially, we took some minor liberties, adding correct punctuation, for example, to aid in readability offline.

If you have the time and desire to count characters in this book, then A) you might want to up your meds or B) you'd probably make an excellent Quality Assurance professional and should consider an immediate career change.

PART 1

WAKE UP!
It's GO Time!

9 a.m. Birds chirping outside yonder window slowly rouse you from your slumber, gently easing you into a bright new morning. Remember those days? Of course you do. You can recall a time when all your mornings were calm and relaxed.

Well, that's all gone to hell now.

These days, you are catapulted into consciousness at 5:30 a.m. as one tot rolls across your neck—*Whoa! That diaper is ripe!*—another small tyrant shrieks in your face and your tween slams around the bathroom because ... oh, who the hell knows. You'd need a flow-chart to keep pace with all the melodramas there.

Welcome to mornings at Every Parent's House, USA!

Mornings should be a simple process: Get 'em up, get 'em fed, get 'em dressed, get 'em out. And yet, quick-marching your small brood through their paces and into the car for school requires laser focus, steely determination and the resilience of a zen master to diffuse the kinds of PDEs (potential domestic explosives) that threaten to blow every morning to smithereens.

Once you've maneuvered through the school drop-off gauntlet though, you might steal a few moments to yourself for indulging in one of life's little luxuries—like completing a sentence or taking a shower—before your pint-sized dictator conscripts you to "play trains" for the longest hour of your life.

Ahhhhh. There's no harm in dreaming, is there?

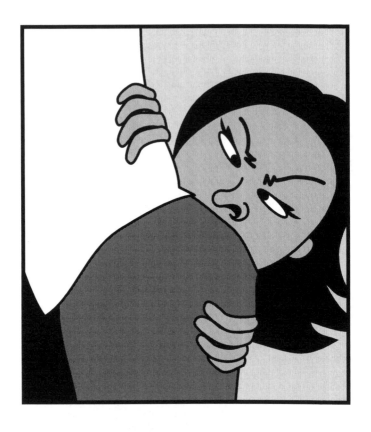

**Being a parent means being willing
to sniff another human's butt in public
to rule out that "the smell"
is not your kid.**

— Jennifer Lizza (@OutsmartedMommy)

Part of the joy of having children is experiencing things anew, from their perspective. Unfortunately, one of those things is the sunrise.

— Dad and Buried (@DadAndBuried)

This morning I held a 2-minute family meeting with a demo entitled: "How to Change a Roll of Toilet Paper." They were in awe of how easy it is.

— Domestic Goddess (@DomesticGoddss)

Pretty sure my son was disappointed in the 30%-off coupon to Bed, Bath & Beyond that the Tooth Fairy left him last night.

— Abe Yospe (@Cheeseboy22)

3yo: *singing in the bathroom* I have to go poopoo. The poopoo is coming out. And it's okay to touch the poo-
Me: *sprints into bathroom*

— Father With Twins (@FatherWithTwins)

Imagine having kids ...
Wrong. You don't have time to imagine anymore.

— Simon Holland (@SimonCHolland)

"OMG! I HATE school this year! The teachers are, like, SO unfair! Seriously, like WHY do we even have to DO it? OMG!"
— Me to my teens

— Housewife of Hell (@HousewifeOfHell)

Hate to be THAT parent, but if I'm up at 5 a.m. on a Saturday for your baseball game, you better win.

— Sarcastic Mommy (@SarcasticMommy4)

I wish someone would leave a horse's head in my bed so that when my kids sneak up on me in the morning, I can be like, "BAM! Horse's head!"

— Kalvin MacLeod (@KalvinMacLeod)

6yo: Why haven't we had breakfast yet?
Me: It's summer, and we're not in a rush.
3yo: What does that mean?
6yo: I guess it means we starve.

— Jennifer Lizza (@OutsmartedMommy)

The baby said, "Hot Mama" 10 times in a row. She was talking about her oatmeal, but I'll take what I can get.

— Jewel Nunez (@OneFunnyMummy)

Kids are just so ... so ... AWAKE in the mornings.

— Jen Good (@BuriedWithKids)

How to calm a crying baby:
1) Pick it up.
2) Ok, so when it turns like, 5, you can put it back down. Good luck.

— Lurk at Home Mom (@LurkAtHomeMom)

Every night I tuck in an adorable 6yo.
Yet every morning,
I drag Keith Richards out of bed.

— Brenna Jennings (@SuburbanSnaps)

Can anyone tell me whether or not my children will like potatoes this week?

— Kalvin MacLeod (@KalvinMacLeod)

Mommy: *gets off the phone* Ugh, I sounded like a douche.
4yo: What's a douche?
Mommy: Nothing.
Me: I gotta go to work.
4yo: Good-bye, douche!

— Father With Twins (@FatherWithTwins)

Cutting a baby's fingernails is like cutting the red, yellow and green wires on a bomb, hoping each clip doesn't set off an explosion.

— The ParentNormal (@ParentNormal)

Letting 7yos make toast was not my best parenting idea.

Related: All the smoke detectors in the house are in great working order.

— Jen Good (@BuriedWithKids)

Not even 8 a.m.
and I've already canceled
Christmas twice.

— Bunmi Laditan (@BunmiLaditan)

There are days that start with a beautiful sunrise, and then there are days that start with mistaking a dead fly for a raisin.

— Stephanie Jankowski (@CrazyExhaustion)

What do a toddler, a preschooler and a pregnant woman all have in common? We all pee our pants in public.

— Chrissy Howe (@FullMetalMommy)

When I realized my new haircut was a "mom" cut, I cried bitter tears of despair onto my Jordache dark-wash elastic-waist jeans.

— Linda Doty (@LindaInDisguise)

5yo: I don't flush in the morning because I'm afraid monsters will hear it. But they won't hear the Mario Bros. game blasting? I see.

— Science of Parenthood (@SciOfParenthood)

Can taking your kids
to Starbucks
count as a craft?

— Bunmi Laditan (@BunmiLaditan)

My son: Garbage trucks take brave men to the scene of the garbage.

Me: ...

— Sarah del Rio (@Est1975Blog)

We were ready for school early, so we let the boys play for a minute or two. And that was enough time for them to completely disrobe.

— David Vienna (@TheDaddyComplex)

Yesterday
I cleaned my house, which is dumb because we still live here.

— Amy Flory (@FunnyIsFamily)

Waiting for 5yo to break Siri with her questions.

— Kathy Cooperman (@Kathy_Cooperman)

5yo: I'm angry!

Me: I know.

5yo: I don't like it when you say that!

Me: Ok.

5yo: I don't like that either!

Me:

5yo: Why aren't you talking to me?!

— Father With Twins (@FatherWithTwins)

Sex Ed for teenagers should include trying to get 2 kids ready for school in the morning.

— Jennifer Lizza (@OutsmartedMommy)

4yo followed me to the bathroom (as usual) & I had to explain menstruation. I think I failed because at the end she asked, "So ... you're dead?"

— Bunmi Laditan (@BunmiLaditan)

I've breastfed 5 kids.
I think the bigger question is who HASN'T seen my boobs.

— Linda Doty (@LindaInDisguise)

Toddlers are great at whispering if whispering means talking as quietly as they shout.

— The ParentNormal (@ParentNormal)

Today is picture day at the boys' school.
Once again, our boys look like they just got
back from an all-night band practice.

— David Vienna (@TheDaddyComplex)

My 2yo's least favorite sippy cup is whichever one I already poured his drink into.

— Lurk at Home Mom (@LurkAtHomeMom)

One minute your kids are babies, and the next you're sleeping in till 9:30 a.m. because they have the iPad and can reach the cereal.

— Amy Flory (@FunnyIsFamily)

The fact that I just angrily yelled "You're not the boss of me!" at my 2yo is a pretty clear indication that he definitely is.

— Dad and Buried (@DadAndBuried)

Me: Hey, buddy, you want some toast for breakfast?
2yo: Beer.
Me: Well, it's 9 a.m., so no. But I hear ya.

— Paige Kellerman (@PaigeKellerman)

"MUMMMMMY! My brudder won't play with me! He keeps playing with himself!"
Get used to it, girl.

— Stephanie Jankowski (@CrazyExhaustion)

My son tripped over a box of Legos and landed on about 185 tiny pieces. I feel like this is 6 years of karma finally catching up with him.

— Bethany Thies (@BPMBadassMama)

"Daddy said I can get a baby hedgehog."
So now I need to get rid of a baby hedgehog
AND Daddy.

— Housewife of Hell (@HousewifeOfHell)

"Hey! I have a great idea! Let's dump out 500 toys all over the floor; fight over 1; and then tell mom we're bored."
— Kids everywhere

— Jennifer Lizza (@OutsmartedMommy)

Me: Found one of your sippy cups, bud.
2yo: I put away.
Me: Thank you, that's a big help!
2yo: Ok. *throws in linen closet and walks away*

— Paige Kellerman (@PaigeKellerman)

I wish bottles of ibuprofen came with a little prize inside, like maybe a babysitter.

— Brenna Jennings (@SuburbanSnaps)

Before I had kids, I didn't even know it was possible to destroy an entire house with a granola bar.

— Lurk at Home Mom (@LurkAtHomeMom)

The boys were fighting over Minecraft so I asked them if they'd like to play a game called Minecrap where they dig for poop in the litter box.

— Domestic Goddess (@DomesticGoddss)

I was singing Billy Idol really loud in the car ("White Wedding"). My 12yo took my imaginary microphone. He also held my hand so I'd stop.

— Days of Wine and Yoda (@FabLife4)

4yo: Did Mommy say it was ok?

Me: Daddy said it was ok, and Daddy's in charge.

4yo: *whispers* Not all the time.

— Father With Twins (@FatherWithTwins)

The key to raising respectful teens is leaving them in the forest forever at age 12.

— So Done Mom (@MomToTeens)

So if you think drunk people are loud, then you have never heard my children yelling at each other to be quiet in the morning.

— Jen Good (@BuriedWithKids)

16yo is spending her summer looking for work, helping around the house, volunteering in the community and sleeping. Except for the first three.

-— Steve Olivas (@SteveOlivas)

All my friends surprising their kids with Disney trips make me feel bad because my kid's surprises mostly involve ambush booster shots.

— Brenna Jennings (@SuburbanSnaps)

We don't ask for much. Just your undivided attention and every scrap of patience.
— Kids

— Jewel Nunez (@OneFunnyMummy)

**I'm at my most *Fast & Furious*
when my 3yo has to suddenly poop
on a crowded freeway.**

— Father With Twins (@FatherWithTwins)

Both 18yo & 16yo: "Leaving for school now. Bye. We love you!"
Me: *waves, smiles & opens the locator app to see where they're really going*

— So Done Mom (@MomToTeens)

I get excited when I think summer vacation is almost here, and then I remember my kids will be home.

— Sarcastic Mommy (@SarcasticMommy4)

My teen daughter dropped her phone. It broke. The world came to an end. Good-bye, everybody.

— Housewife of Hell (@HousewifeOfHell)

Within 60 seconds of my kids being in a room, it looks like 100 monkeys have been living in it for 10 years.

— Bethany Thies (@BPMBadassMama)

Dad: Do you love your little sister?
10yo: About 4.5.
Dad: No, it's not on a scale of 1 to 10.
10yo: That was a scale of 1 to 100.

— Kate Hall (@KateWhineHall)

I always thought winning an Oscar must be really hard until I became a parent and faked interest in a 2-hour story about a bug on a leaf.

— Jennifer Lizza (@OutsmartedMommy)

5yo found some of his art in the trash, so today I'll be out buying a pony.

— Amy Flory (@FunnyIsFamily)

4yo: *shoots me with gun*
stuffs gun in my pocket
runs away
Me: *Realizes he just made it look like a suicide*
keeping an eye on him

— Father With Twins (@FatherWithTwins)

I'm always so proud of how my kids go green and repurpose their old arguments so they work for today.

— Paige Kellerman (@PaigeKellerman)

Hell hath no fury like a 4yo
whose sandwich has been cut into squares
when he wanted triangles.

— Lurk at Home Mom (@LurkAtHomeMom)

The key to successfully pawning a whiny toddler off on your wife is making sure she doesn't hear you say, "Go see what Mommy's doing!"

— Dad and Buried (@DadAndBuried)

"That's it! You just lost your Lucky Charms privileges!"
— Me, running out of parenting options

— The Walking Dad (@RealDMK)

I like to do the gym stairclimber for an hour then come home and stand at the foot of the stairs screaming, "Don't make me come up there!"

— So Done Mom (@MomToTeens)

> My 10yo son has committed to wearing only one shoe today, in honor of losing the other one.
>
> — Steve Olivas (@SteveOlivas)

4yo: Mom!

Me: What?

4yo: I can't get my head to come off!

Me: Pull harder, honey.

4yo: Ok!

Me:

4yo: Ow!

Me: *looks up from phone* Wait, what?

— Lurk at Home Mom (@LurkAtHomeMom)

"Do your LEGO mini figures ever just go and have coffee?"
8yo ignores me & keeps making them kick each other in the face

— Kelley Nettles (@KelleysBreakRm)

My 4yo is trying to sell my own M&M's back to me. This guy's going places.

— Father With Twins (@FatherWithTwins)

"One day, son, this will all be yours."
points to two pennies and a nickel found in dryer lint trap

— Housewife of Hell (@HousewifeOfHell)

5yo: When I'm a mommy, I'm not gonna make my kids take baths or eat healthy. And I'm gonna name 'em Stinky, Fatty & Donut.

— Kathy Cooperman (@Kathy_Cooperman)

Thanks to our daily struggle to get the kids out the door in the morning, when things go smoothly, I feel unsettled.

— David Vienna (@TheDaddyComplex)

Ok, kids. Does everyone have their shoes, socks, snacks, books, diapers, fights and questions about mortality? Good, let's run errands.

— Paige Kellerman (@PaigeKellerman)

My toddler is quite sophisticated. She holds her pinky finger out when she spills orange juice all over herself.

— The ParentNormal (@ParentNormal)

Me: *gets on scale*
5yo: Whoa! That's a lot of points!

— Kate Hall (@KateWhineHall)

My boys called me on my threat to take things away when they misbehave, so now they're playing with tree bark, and we live in a yurt.

— David Vienna (@TheDaddyComplex)

You can't call yourself a mom until you've tried to poop faster because a kid is screaming at you from the other room.

— One Funny Mummy (@OneFunnyMummy)

9yo: Can I get a cell phone? I need to be able to talk to people.
Me: No. You can use a soup can and string like a normal kid.

— Jen Good (@BuriedWithKids)

Like Shakira, my hips don't lie. Hers say, "I'm so sexy!" Mine say, "I like cheese and birthing babies."

— Bethany Thies (@BPMBadassMama)

"DADDY! MY BOOGERS HURT!"

And I'm not exactly sure how I'm supposed to respond to that.

— Andy H. (@AndyAsAdjective)

> Just saved $25
> on a flu shot by having my
> 7yo sneeze in my face.
>
> — Abe Yospe (@Cheeseboy22)

Things my kids give me on Father's Day:

1) Grief

2) Attitude

3) Malaise

4) A card Mom bought and forced them to sign.

— Steve Olivas (@SteveOlivas)

When stopped at a DUI checkpoint and an officer asks if I've been drinking, is it inappropriate to answer, "I WISH"?

— Stephanie Jankowski (@CrazyExhaustion)

My son just referred to the 1980s as "turn of the century."

— Sarah del Rio (@Est1975Blog)

With my wife away, my children keep asking me for things like meals and Band-Aids and sympathy, but I don't know where we keep any of that.

— Kalvin MacLeod (@KalvinMacLeod)

Nothing screams "I'm a parent" more than pulling out your wallet in the checkout line along with a pair of Power Ranger underwear.

— Jennifer Lizza (@OutsmartedMommy)

My version of winning at board games with my kids is being the first one eliminated.

— Linda Doty (@LindaInDisguise)

"Oh, we're leaving now? Ok. Gimme one sec. I just need to take off my shoes and throw a tantrum about cupcakes. Then we can go."
— My 2yo

— Lurk at Home Mom (@LurkAtHomeMom)

We have cute nicknames for each of our 2 kids. We call the 1st "The one who gets up at 5 a.m. EVERY day" and the other "The one we don't hate."

— Andy H. (@AndyAsAdjective)

16yo is playing this game with me called The Silent Treatment.

He thinks he's winning. Rookie.

— Sarcastic Mommy (@SarcasticMommy4)

My kids have one of those Sit 'n Spins, but since they never listen, it is basically a Stand 'n Fall.

— Simon Holland (@SimonCHolland)

**To anyone out there thinking about
having kids, today my 2yo threw
a temper tantrum because she couldn't
get rid of her shadow.**

— Exploding Unicorn (@XplodingUnicorn)

3yo to 5yo: Try to tackle me, and then I'll tackle you! Use that bat!

If you need me, we'll be at the emergency room.

— Stephanie Jankowski (@CrazyExhaustion)

Kids are like drinks. You never realize you've had too many until that last one, and by then it's too late.

— Linda Doty (@LindaInDisguise)

Oh thank God she finally stopped screaming and brought the kids inside. That lady is insane.

— My neighbors

— Chrissy Howe (@FullMetalMommy)

My kids are pretty advanced. They are already ignoring me at a 5th grade level.

— Father With Twins (@FatherWithTwins)

How to tell if your 2yo is about to melt down over something:

1) He's awake.

— Lurk at Home Mom (@LurkAtHomeMom)

Put a new blender on your baby registry. It drowns out the crying and makes margaritas. You're welcome.

— Jewel Nunez (@OneFunnyMummy)

Me: You sound like a broken record.

3yo: What's that?

Me: It's an old type of CD.

3yo: What's a CD?

Me: *moves into a nursing home*

— Exploding Unicorn (@XplodingUnicorn)

Kids: the best thing that's ever happened to you that you occasionally wish had never happened to you.

— Dad and Buried (@DadAndBuried)

PART 2

Afternoon Delight? Yeah, Right.

What do parents really need? Yeah, yeah ... infinite patience and boundless love are nice. The ability to function on mere minutes of sleep is helpful, and a gift subscription to the Wine-Of-The-Month Club is definitely appreciated. But to make it through the Tough Mudder/ IronMan event that is childrearing, parents especially need the following:

A philosophical outlook on life.

The ability to multitask like IBM's Deep Blue computer.

A full tank of gas.

Because once you get past the feeding and the wiping and the potty-training stages, most of parenting really comes down to fielding those Big Questions—*What happens when you die? Why can't we get a kangaroo? Why don't mommies have penises?*—while simultaneously opening snacks, making work calls, mentally racking your brain for what you could possibly make for dinner and criss-crossing town to get the kids from school to soccer, the tutor, scouts, dance class, and *if you're really lucky* ... the grocery store. (Because *What's for dinner?* remains YOUR Big Question.)

Still, you might keep a fully charged iPad on hand as well. You'll need *something* to keep the kiddos occupied when it's finally time to tap that Big Box O' Chardonnay. What time IS it, anyway? Oh, what the hell. It's always 5 p.m. somewhere. Salud!

I just sucked melted chocolate off my 2yo's filthy fingers, in case you're from the future and wondering how the outbreak started.

— Dad and Buried (@DadAndBuried)

I can't be expected to foster a love of reading in my children AND remember the diaper bag. I'm only 1 woman.

— Bunmi Laditan (@BunmiLaditan)

My son's superpower is to turn 1 cracker into 10 lbs. of crumbs.

— Father With Twins (@FatherWithTwins)

Dear Children, I've been flushing toilets for over 30 years. I know how and don't need any more practice. Love, Mom

— Jen Good (@BuriedWithKids)

Sits on playground bench.

Watches kid 1.

Looks around for kid 2.

Panics.

Sees kid 2.

Looks for kid 1.

Panics.

Sees kid 1.

Looks for kid 2.

Panics.

— Lurk at Home Mom (@LurkAtHomeMom)

Yes, ladies, you CAN
have it all!
But keep in mind,
most of it sucks.

— Housewife of Hell (@HousewifeOfHell)

Problem of the Day: If a mom has 0 kids and 2 hours of free time, how long will she sit in the car looking at Twitter before entering Target?

— Jewel Nunez (@OneFunnyMummy)

Just in case anyone is looking for their snot, my son has it all over his face. All of it.

MY SON HAS ALL THE SNOT.

— Dad and Buried (@DadAndBuried)

My 7yo daughter cautioning her 9yo brother: "When you get married, some girl will boss you about where to put a couch."

— Kathy Cooperman (@Kathy_Cooperman)

Me: Time to go to the library.

4yo: *runs, grabs sword*

Me: You need that for the library?

4yo: Yes.

Me:

4yo:

Me: Ok, let's go.

— Father With Twins (@FatherWithTwins)

4yo: I used the potty. Can I have a treat?

Me: No. You always go in the potty.

4yo: I can stop.

Me:

Apparently I negotiate with terrorists.

— Exploding Unicorn (@XplodingUnicorn)

If you think you can ride your kid's Razor scooter over the curb dip of your driveway without severe injury, you're an idiot. I'm an idiot.

— Andy H. (@AndyAsAdjective)

My kids love
juice boxes, unless someone else
puts the straw in.
THEN THEY'RE RUINED.

— Amy Flory (@FunnyIsFamily)

You say your dog won't bite, but that's just because you haven't seen how hard my toddler can pull a tail.

— The ParentNormal (@ParentNormal)

I just completed 6 different activities with my 5yo, but that's only taken up 30 minutes of the day.

— Kate Hall (@KateWhineHall)

My wife & daughters are away at the beach all week, leaving me home alone. In just one day we've already saved $6,000 in toilet paper.

— Andy H. (@AndyAsAdjective)

My kids are quiet.
I think they are reloading.

— Kathy Cooperman (@Kathy_Cooperman)

"By the way, Mom, Daddy is taking me back-to-school shopping instead of you. He gives me more money and less chit-chat."

— Housewife of Hell (@HousewifeOfHell)

I can't eat this sleeve of Oreos fast enough.
Seriously, the kids are coming,
and they can't know we have these.

— Amy Flory (@FunnyIsFamily)

"How much for the baby slingshot?"

"Ma'am, that's a swing set."

"I'll take 2."

"And how much for the toddler cages?"

"That's a playhouse."

— Lurk at Home Mom (@LurkAtHomeMom)

I leave more parties with a girl crying in my backseat than a limo driver on prom night.

— Brenna Jennings (@SuburbanSnaps)

Me: Ok, Mommy is sick & it's spring break. Here're the keys. Go somewhere for 4 hours. Them: We don't know how to drive. Me: Bring home dinner, too.

— Days of Wine and Yoda (@FabLife4)

They say it takes a village to raise a child. That's why some days I drop my kids off in the middle of a village.

— Abe Yospe (@Cheeseboy22)

Me: What was your favorite part of the movie?
3yo: The hand dryer in the bathroom was awesome!
6yo: Hey! I didn't get to go to the bathroom!

— Jennifer Lizza (@OutsmartedMommy)

I hope by the time my youngest is ready for college, they offer Minecraft scholarships.

— Linda Doty (@LindaInDisguise)

Sitting in car line. Braless. In sweatpants, with broken elastic. Listening to "I Want You" by Savage Garden. I have no regrets.

— Sarah del Rio (@Est1975Blog)

Parenting tip:
Always yell, "I WILL TURN THIS CAR AROUND!" whenever you have to do a U-turn.

— Abe Yospe (@Cheeseboy22)

My 4yo just shut the bathroom door on me while I was inside and told me I was in jail. So I locked the door. I love this game.

— Kate Hall (@KateWhineHall)

Hardest thing about writing about parenting is knowing when to yell at the kids to be quiet so I can write about what a great parent I am.

— Paige Kellerman (@PaigeKellerman)

Convo overheard from the backseat:
"Sometimes I stick random stuff in my p..."
(nonononononono)
"...piggy bank"
(OHTHANKGOD)

— Science of Parenthood (@SciOfParenthood)

Just paid my 7yo son $2 to shut up & do his homework & then another dollar not to tell his mom I gave him $2 to do his homework.

— Abe Yospe (@Cheeseboy22)

Saves 2 cookies for kids.

Eats 1 cookie.

Saves 1 cookie for kids.

Eats half a cookie.

Eats other half.

Never mentions the cookies again.

— Kalvin MacLeod (@KalvinMacLeod)

Just read that the average cost of raising a child is $250K — and that's just Legos.

— Domestic Goddess (@DomesticGoddss)

WHY AM I ALIVE?! And other grateful things my kids say when they see what I've bought at the grocery store.

— Sarcastic Mommy (@SarcasticMommy4)

2yo said, "Worst day EVER!"
while eating ice cream in the sun on her
monogrammed towel.
I hope with time and therapy she'll be ok.

— Bethany Thies (@BPMBadassMama)

Let's get married and have kids so instead of doing fun stuff on the weekend we can go to a kid's birthday party where everyone coughs.

— Simon Holland (@SimonCHolland)

I never feel
as close to another mom
as when she backs me up in a lie
I told my kid.

— Bunmi Laditan (@BunmiLaditan)

My artistic 3yo has chosen the dining room table as her canvas, a blue Sharpie as her paintbrush & lax supervision as her motivation.

— Andy H. (@AndyAsAdjective)

I just threatened to send my kids outside if they couldn't get along playing video games, and I'm not qualified for any of this.

— Kalvin MacLeod (@KalvinMacLeod)

If this kid's not gonna nap, then she needs to get a job.

— Jewel Nunez (@OneFunnyMummy)

Gave my kids a history lesson today: Saw a pay phone. They took turns listening to the dial tone. Taught them how to call grandma collect.

— Kate Hall (@KateWhineHall)

I see you watching me drive by in my 2004 minivan filled with car seats & trash. I bet you're wondering what it feels like to have it all.

— Bethany Thies (@BPMBadassMama)

Kid 1: What are sex slaves?
Kid 2: Yeah, what ARE sex slaves??
And that will conclude today's play date.

— Science of Parenthood (@SciOfParenthood)

Glad my son can read because now someone calls out from the backseat every 2 minutes with the current speed limit and how I'm exceeding it.

— Kate Hall (@KateWhineHall)

I'm glad I just spent 1,000 hours putting together a Lego thing my 6yo will destroy in 5 sec ... Oh.
2 seconds.

— Sarah del Rio (@Est1975Blog)

Help! My wife made me push a double stroller into a Gymboree at the mall, and I've been stuck in here since May.

— Simon Holland (@SimonCHolland)

I never realized
how easily I embarrass until
I had kids who could talk.

— Jennifer Lizza (@OutsmartedMommy)

My kid just ran full force into the wall because he wanted to. Twice. I'm just gonna start using his college fund to buy wine.

— Jen Good (@BuriedWithKids)

I only have to wait 30 more years before my daughter realizes I know what I'm talking about.

— Jewel Nunez (@OneFunnyMummy)

Can differentiate between the sounds of toddler pissing on floor and juice box being squeezed out on floor.

updates resume

— Lurk at Home Mom (@LurkAtHomeMom)

3yo: I am agnostic!
Grandma: YOU ARE A CATHOLIC!
Me: Relax, Mom. She said "exhausted."

— Stephanie Jankowski (@CrazyExhaustion)

I'm at my parenting best when I randomly yell out, "Be careful!" every few minutes without looking up from my phone.

— Dad and Buried (@DadAndBuried)

Took the boys to the beach & heard 6yo yell to a little girl, "You have crabs? Cool!" Please let that be the only time he says that to a girl.

— Domestic Goddess (@DomesticGoddss)

5yo: Mom, will you get me a yogurt?
Me: You're closer to the fridge.
5yo: *moves to the other side of the room*
Now you're closer.

— Amy Flory (@FunnyIsFamily)

Budgeting Tip #105:
Put 3 kids in your shopping cart so
you only have room for bread and milk.
The end.

— Paige Kellerman (@PaigeKellerman)

Don't do that. Kids will make fun of you. But don't worry what others think because you have to be your own man. Ugh, parenting is stupid.

— Kalvin MacLeod (@KalvinMacLeod)

Signed my kid up for karate class a month ago, and he hasn't waxed my car once.

— Abe Yospe (@Cheeseboy22)

Watched my 4yo make a potato chip sandwich with cookies for the bread, and now he's my new life coach.

— Father With Twins (@FatherWithTwins)

If Joe has 6 apples, and Madge takes 4, what is Madge's emotional IQ? Will the principal call Madge's mom? Do they know that Joe eats paste?

— Housewife of Hell (@HousewifeOfHell)

My son, to the stewardess: Thank you for the flight. I really enjoyed it.
My son, to me: Your breath smells.

— Sarah del Rio (@Est1975Blog)

When you're a parent, Festivus is every day at 3pm when you pick the kids up from school & the airing of grievances commences.

— Domestic Goddess (@DomesticGoddss)

Parents who hover while their kids play at the park: Get a Twitter account and sit down.

— Jen Good (@BuriedWithKids)

How to get a kiddie pop-up tent back into the box:

1) Place foot on tent.

2) Twist.

3) Fold.

4) Light on fire.

5) Pour ashes into box.

— Lurk at Home Mom (@LurkAtHomeMom)

Had to take my son's toys from him
& play with them myself. Sorry, but there's
no way a triceratops beats a T. rex in a fight.
Now stop crying.

—— The Walking Dad (@RealDMK)

I've been "invited" to a meeting at my son's school today. That's the educational system's version of "Honey, we have to talk."

— Housewife of Hell (@HousewifeOfHell)

I don't always vacation with kids, but when I do, I wish I had left them at home.

— Sarcastic Mommy (@SarcasticMommy4)

Having kids is just like winning the lottery except you LOSE tons of money, and everyone you've ever met suddenly wants NOTHING to do with you.

— Dad and Buried (@DadAndBuried)

Job interview

What can our company do for you?

Me: Wow. OMG. I ... Ok, kids, come on in. Thanks. If you could just watch them for an hour ...

— Lurk at Home Mom (@LurkAtHomeMom)

My daughter told me
I'm "slightly prettier than Ben
Franklin."
So I have that going for me.

— Housewife of Hell (@HousewifeOfHell)

75% of parenting is spent acting like you are super-excited for the answer after your kid says "You know what, Mommy?" for the 800th time.

— Jennifer Lizza (@OutsmartedMommy)

This mom is running around the playground with her kids. I'm watching mine from the car while I tweet and think about marshmallows.

— Kate Hall (@KateWhineHall)

Listen Kid, I already DID all my own homework, and handed it in a long, long time ago. NOW IT'S YOUR TURN.

— Housewife of Hell (@HousewifeOfHell)

**World peace could be achieved
if all the political leaders of the world
had to work together to
dress and undress Barbies.**

— Danielle Herzog (@MartinisAndMini)

I go full-on hostage negotiator when I see my 3yo holding a permanent marker without the lid.

— Simon Holland (@SimonCHolland)

The 6yo just rolled
her eyes at me so hard
I could hear it.

— Brenna Jennings (@SuburbanSnaps)

Parenting is all fun & games until your 3yo pees in the garbage pail instead of the toilet. Then it's just a fraternity party with no beer.

— Jennifer Lizza (@OutsmartedMommy)

If you're having a bad parenting day & see me staring, I'm not judging you. I'm thinking, "Thank God I'm not the only one who sucks at this."

— Jennifer Lizza (@OutsmartedMommy)

I swear, my kids will make me drive them to my own funeral. And then to the mall.

— Housewife of Hell (@HousewifeOfHell)

She took 4yo to the park & texted, "Can I get her ice cream?"

Get her a Heineken for all I care. Free babysitters get to call the shots.

— Bunmi Laditan (@BunmiLaditan)

You will only forget to knock before entering once.

— Teen Parenting

— So Done Mom (@MomToTeens)

Fun Fact: The average group of 4yos can take up to 7 years to break open a piñata.

— Lurk at Home Mom (@LurkAtHomeMom)

Having 3 kids means sometimes you eat out and forget to order a meal for 1, and they remind you of that every time you eat out until you die.

— Kate Hall (@KateWhineHall)

**Youngest discovered an old harmonica
at my parents house.
I discovered yet another uncharted
circle of hell.**

— Domestic Goddess (@DomesticGoddss)

Imagine how much MORE money we would spend if they put a bar in Target? Damn it, I should be in marketing focus groups.

— Danielle Herzog (@MartinisAndMini)

Son had a fight with a friend yesterday. An hour later they were fine.

Daughter had a fight with a friend 9 years ago. They still don't speak.

— Steve Olivas (@SteveOlivas)

We're at the top of the 34th inning at this little kid softball game. Wait. No ... wait. I stand corrected. Top of the 2nd.

— Linda Doty (@LindaInDisguise)

Sons laughing

Me: *Walks into bathroom*

One son sitting on toilet, other son trying to pee in between his legs

Me: *Walks out of room*

— Father With Twins (@FatherWithTwins)

15yo: Can I have a ride to my boyfriend's house?

Me: Sure! I just need to show you this video first.

puts on video of a natural childbirth

— So Done Mom (@MomToTeens)

You know it'll be an interesting day when your kid asks what porn is, and then you realize she said "mourn" AFTER you just explained porn.

— Danielle Herzog (@MartinisAndMini)

Living with a 4yo is like watching someone fill out a MadLib and just put "NO!" in every single spot.

— Dad and Buried (@DadAndBuried)

I just saw a family with 4 very unhappy adolescents at a highway rest stop. I've seen my future, and it's everything I dreamed it would be.

— Bethany Thies (@BPMBadassMama)

Yes, my car has stick figure decals of my kids on the rear window. I'm not bragging. I'm warning people.

— Kathy Cooperman (@Kathy_Cooperman)

My wife: That's not the shirt I sent her to daycare in.
Me: But it's the right kid?
Wife: Yes.
Me: Awesome. I'm going to play Xbox.

— Exploding Unicorn (@XplodingUnicorn)

You two go ahead and kill each other. I'm gonna stand here and eat all the Rice Krispy treats.

— Jewel Nunez (@OneFunnyMummy)

MMM. My lunch tastes like maternal superiority and the tears of inadequate moms who packed PB&Js with the crusts on.
–Kid with Bento Box

— Chrissy Howe (@FullMetalMommy)

Just saw a 3yo girl fighting with her brother while wearing "World's Greatest Sister" shirt. I'm guessing he didn't pick that one out.

— Kate Hall (@KateWhineHall)

Seeing your has-been-an-obnoxious-jerk-all-day 4yo suddenly break into a yawn is like finding a twenty in your jeans.

— Dad and Buried (@DadAndBuried)

If you say "Look what they turn into!" and show everyone your college kids' Instagram pics, you won't have to go to baby showers anymore.

— So Done Mom (@MomToTeens)

Cashier: Need to see some ID.

Me: You get a lot of 20yo guys buying tampons, diapers, grapes & whiskey?

Cashier: Yup.

Me: Ok, here you go then.

— Father With Twins (@FatherWithTwins)

Today my 4yo was so tired she could barely keep her eyes open. Then she slept for 86 seconds in the car and will now be up forever.

— Simon Holland (@SimonCHolland)

On my son's homework, he was supposed to fill in letters to complete a word: _ _ at. He wrote "shat."

I swear, I almost shat my pants.

— Bethany Thies (@BPMBadassMama)

Parenthood is simply an increasingly ridiculous escalation of threats until you've taken away the possibility of having a pet llama.

— Kalvin MacLeod (@KalvinMacLeod)

PART 3

The Bitching Hours

There is nothing quite like the dulcet tones of whiny, bickering children (*He's touching me! She's breathing on me! Stop looking at me!*) to ring in the evening. Ah, the witching hour, or as parents call it, the "bitching hour" (or *hours*). That in-between time after school and before bed when hunger is high, patience is thin and fuses are very, very short.

You can try to minimize the meltdowns, of

course, but between you and the children, that really is a lot to ask. Or maybe you lucked out and have kids who settle right in to do all of their homework, unassisted, while eating healthy snacks so you can prepare dinner in peace. If so, best keep that to yourself or no one will talk to you at school parties. Ever.

As for dinner ... a check of the pantry yields ... what? Rice noodles, olives and alfredo sauce? Is that all you have?!? Pizza it is, then. At least no one will complain about what you're serving (though they could surprise you).

At long last, it's finally time for bed. Sure, it's only 6:30 p.m., but you know what they say, "Early to bed, early to ... " Oh, screw it. You just want to lie down. And the bedtime process is long, and you are tired. So ... bath. Pajamas. Teeth. Story. Song. Water. Story. Song. Bathroom. Monster-check. Water.

Bathroom. Another story. One more song ...

Finally ... quiet.

Ha-ha! We're kidding, of course! Count on repeating the above routine at least twice for each child, until you pass out from sheer exhaustion in one of their beds, rendering you (blissfully) deaf to their plaintive requests for more stories, songs, water ...

Sleep tight, Parents. Because you get to do it all over again tomorrow.

This margarita tastes like I don't even have kids.

— Kate Hall (@KateWhineHall)

There should be a theme park called Parentland where only parents can go. The rides would be couches where parents can just sit in peace.

— Abe Yospe (@Cheeseboy22)

Highlights from tonight's soccer:
Wedgies picked: 6
Noses picked: 4
Goals made: 0
Only 1 more hour to go.

— Domestic Goddess (@DomesticGoddss)

I can't tell if my toddler is TERRIBLE at speaking ... or AMAZING at beatboxing.

— Dad and Buried (@DadAndBuried)

"This towel rack holds a towel, so that must mean I can hang from it."
— Kids

— Kate Hall (@KateWhineHall)

Kids are like sponges.
They smell bad.

— Bunmi Laditan (@BunmiLaditan)

You could make dinner for a toddler, or you could just cut out the middle man & throw away a plate of food & squirt ketchup on the dog.

— Simon Holland (@SimonCHolland)

Tonight we will be having "That looks kinda yucky" with a side of "How many bites do I have to take?"

— Amy Flory (@FunnyIsFamily)

4yo: What's a tantrum?
Wife: Kids throw them when they're mad.
Me: And some adults. *sideways glance at wife*
Me: *wakes up in the trunk of a car*

— Kalvin MacLeod (@KalvinMacLeod)

The 4yo just told Daddy that she wishes he was a fireman. Listen Kid, no one wishes that more than Mommy.

— Bethany Thies (@BPMBadassMama)

Wife: The baby is crying.

Me: That's a factual statement.

Wife:

Me:

Wife: PICK UP THE BABY!

I'm not a mind reader.

— Exploding Unicorn (@XplodingUnicorn)

Hey restaurants,
how about a
pay-per-bite kids menu?

— Kalvin MacLeod (@KalvinMacLeod)

**Pro tip: Singing along loudly
when your son's friends are in the car
means he'll never ask you to drive again.**

— Sarcastic Mommy (@SarcasticMommy4)

How to ensure a sleepless Christmas Eve:
Child: Do you know how Santa fattens up?
Me: By eating all the bad children?

— Science of Parenthood (@SciOfParenthood)

If you want to find out things like, say, you have food in your teeth or that "you're the worst person ever," get yourself a teenage girl.

— Housewife of Hell (@HousewifeOfHell)

There's nothing sweeter than returning home from a long trip, opening the front door and having your kid look at you and scream, "Noooo!!!"

— Chrissy Howe (@FullMetalMommy)

"Oh my God, I have to make dinner ... AGAIN?!"
— Me, every single day

— Days of Wine and Yoda (@FabLife4)

4yo: *hands me a beer*

Me: Did you shake it?

4yo: No.

Me: *gets drenched by a beer geyser*

4yo: I dropped it down the stairs.

— Exploding Unicorn (@XplodingUnicorn)

My 8yo: I love you, Mom.

Me: Awww!! Why did you say that?

Him: Because ... um, I have no idea. Can I play with your iPhone?

— Kelley Nettles (@KelleysBreakRm)

I'm just like Angelina Jolie in that I wear my children's art. Except it's on my body. In the form of stretch marks.

— Bunmi Laditan (@BunmiLaditan)

All of my experiences and abilities led to the moment when my child asked about farts, and I could punctuate the answer with an actual fart.

— David Vienna (@TheDaddyComplex)

The amount of drama happening
at the dinner table because I'm making
my kids eat salmon makes an
episode of *Real Housewives* look tame.

— Jen Good (@BuriedWithKids)

When it comes down to it, parenting is basically snuggling and watching everything you've ever owned gradually be destroyed.

— Kate Hall (@KateWhineHall)

Me: Eat your food.

8yo: Why? Pizza's not even healthy.

Me: Yes it is. It's cheese & bread, which is calcium & bread JUST EAT YOUR FOOD.

— Bunmi Laditan (@BunmiLaditan)

Anytime I cannot find my kids, I just go to the bathroom and wait for them to barge in.

— The Walking Dad (@RealDMK)

My 7yo has been practicing arm farts —punctuated by cartwheels—for the past 10 minutes. Harvard, save a space!

— Kathy Cooperman (@Kathy_Cooperman)

If I've learned anything since becoming a father, it's that dads are so much better at ignoring stuff than moms.

— Abe Yospe (@Cheeseboy22)

I overheard this man say, "Whenever we make salad for the kids, they just love it."

I hate him.

— Kate Hall (@KateWhineHall)

I just finished
my kid's math homework.
It's wrong, but it's done.

— Jen Good (@BuriedWithKids)

4yo: Grown-ups can do what they want.

Me: Yup.

4yo: Why don't you eat pizza for every meal?

Me:

4yo:

Me: *takes a hard look at my life*

— Exploding Unicorn (@XplodingUnicorn)

For someone who tried to put his shirt on through the arm hole this morning, the 2yo sure bosses me around a lot.

— Paige Kellerman (@PaigeKellerman)

My sons consider "It's bedtime" my first offer in the negotiation process.

— Father With Twins (@FatherWithTwins)

Just had THE TALK with my son. It's confusing. See, episode 4 is really episode 1. Leia didn't know Luke was her brother. Yes, Yoda just quit.

— The Walking Dad (@RealDMK)

Reasons my 2yo threw a fit today:

1) I woke her up.

2) Her socks felt funny.

3) Her balloon was too floaty.

— Exploding Unicorn (@XplodingUnicorn)

Son: "canwepppaaahggwrr."
Me: What?
Son: "canwepppaaahggwrr."
Me: What?
Son: "canwepppaaahggwrr."
Me: Um … sure. Whatever.
Son: Daddy said yes!!
Uh oh

— The Walking Dad (@RealDMK)

Weeee!
Just made it down the slide
without spilling my wine.

— So Done Mom (@MomToTeens)

Sexy used to be him bringing me flowers. Now it's when he reminds the kids to use the bathroom before we leave the house.

— Amy Flory (@FunnyIsFamily)

At the hotel:
Me: I can't leave you in the room alone. You couldn't find us.
7yo: I'd just run down to the bar.
Ahhh, fair enough.

— Science of Parenthood (@SciOfParenthood)

Just me, 17yo daughter, and her phone at home. The three of us may go to dinner later, but I feel like I'm intruding.

— Steve Olivas (@SteveOlivas)

Things yelled by parents tonight:

"Run the other way!"

"Put your shoe back on!"

"No, there aren't snacks at practice!"

"Are you asleep?"

— Domestic Goddess (@DomesticGoddss)

Adore. Lose patience.
Feel guilty. Repeat.
– Parenting

— The Walking Dad (@RealDMK)

My 5yo girl just asked to do my hair. I asked her how it looked when it was done. Her reply: "I can only do so much." Worst salon ever.

— Danielle Herzog (@MartinisAndMini)

Once I realized that fart jokes will crack up an entire room of 9yos, I've looked forward to my son's hockey practices.

— Steve Olivas (@SteveOlivas)

If my husband and I were cops, I'd be the bad cop, and he'd be the get-the-kids-really-hyper-before-bed-so-that-it's-hard-for-them-to-wake-up cop.

— Kelley Nettles (@KelleysBreakRm)

New slogan idea for Band-Aid:
Adhesive bandages for some actual injuries
but mostly the imagined ones.

— The ParentNormal (@ParentNormal)

My husband is in charge of grilling & my kids are in charge of setting the table. I suspect we will be eating burnt chicken with our hands.

— Jennifer Lizza (@OutsmartedMommy)

Well, that hamper is 5 feet away, and the lid is closed, so I'll just shove these dirty clothes under my bed until I outgrow them.
— Kids

— Kate Hall (@KateWhineHall)

Ok, we only have to put them back in their rooms 35 more times, and it's bedtime.
— How husband and I get ready to relax

— Paige Kellerman (@PaigeKellerman)

4yo: There's a shark in my closet.

Me: He'd die without water.

4yo: Then he's a ghost shark.

Me: *stays the hell away from the closet*

— Exploding Unicorn (@XplodingUnicorn)

Me: *jogs by house*
Me: *hears kids whining to husband*
Me: *jogs another 15 miles*

— Lurk at Home Mom (@LurkAtHomeMom)

When Mom goes out:

Gets sitter.

Feeds kids.

Finds 2nd sitter when 1st cancels.

Wipes tears.

Calls home 3 times.

When Dad goes out:

He goes out.

— Housewife of Hell (@HousewifeOfHell)

One Fish, Two Fish, Red Fish,
Go the Hell to Bed Fish.

— Bethany Thies (@BPMBadassMama)

6yo: I'm not sleeping tonight. I'm afraid aliens are going to come take me.
Me: Well, if you're not sleeping tonight, I hope they come take me.

— Jennifer Lizza (@OutsmartedMommy)

If you see me sleeping in my car, don't feel bad for me. I'm not homeless; just trying to get the eff away from my kids.

— Jewel Nunez (@OneFunnyMummy)

One day I'll walk into the kitchen to cook; the pot I need will be clean; the counters empty; and the homeowners will call the cops on me.

— Brenna Jennings (@SuburbanSnaps)

**Restaurants should really just
set the table on fire
after my family leaves it.**

— Kelley Nettles (@KelleysBreakRm)

Today, in Toddler Court:

Judge: The plaintiff says you broke the corner off his cracker.

Me: Yes.

Judge: *bangs gavel* Life without parole.

— Paige Kellerman (@PaigeKellerman)

Me: Did you boys brush your teeth?

Boys (in unison): Yes.

Me: Let me clarify: Did you brush them tonight?

stampede to bathroom

Every damn night.

— Domestic Goddess (@DomesticGoddss)

I hate it when I go to hide out from my kids in the walk-in closet and my husband is already in there hiding out from me.

— Sarcastic Mommy (@SarcasticMommy4)

I'll put the kids to bed.
— Married sext

— Sarah del Rio (@Est1975Blog)

My son just announced he wants to be a zoologist spy when he grows up, and I immediately felt stupid for pursuing a career in marketing.

— David Vienna (@TheDaddyComplex)

Tiger mother, burning bright
What's the homework for tonight?
While my kids chill and watch TV,
Yours slog through fearsome chemistry.

— Housewife of Hell (@HousewifeOfHell)

Reassured the 5yo at 2 a.m. that there are
no werewolves, then went back to bed where
I can't let my feet hang over because of the
evil clowns.

— Brenna Jennings (@SuburbanSnaps)

Me: What does everyone want for dinner?
Them: Whatever you feel like making.
2 hours later: *everyone goes to Chipotle*

— So Done Mom (@MomToTeens)

I snuck in a nice nap
during the time it took 9yo son
to explain this Xbox game to me.

— Steve Olivas (@SteveOlivas)

If they gave Oscars for Best Actor in a Dinner-Time Drama, the 6yo would snare it for his performance of the Broccoli Consumption Torture.

— Science of Parenthood (@SciOfParenthood)

Going out on a date with my husband tonight. Still deciding if we'll converse with or ignore the three kids tagging along.

— Kate Hall (@KateWhineHall)

I took the "What Kind of Parent Are You?" Facebook quiz, and my results came back "The Kind That Ignores Your Kids While you Take Quizzes."

— Abe Yospe (@Cheeseboy22)

I bet if
Bruce Banner had children
he'd be the Hulk
more than 90% of the time.

— Kalvin MacLeod (@KalvinMacLeod)

4yo: My teacher said zombies aren't real.

Me: That sounds like something a zombie would say.

4yo: *hides under her bed forever*

— Exploding Unicorn (@XplodingUnicorn)

I foster proper social skills during family dinners by insisting everyone share something interesting they are reading on their devices.

— So Done Mom (@MomToTeens)

We're trying to decide what to do for family vacation this summer. Personally, I'd like to go into my room and shut the door for a week.

— Steve Olivas (@SteveOlivas)

My 9yo said she always unbuttons her jeans when she sits on the couch because I do. So that's my legacy right there, people.

— Linda Doty (@LindaInDisguise)

I spray deodorant
on my 12yo son while he's sleeping.
You're welcome.

— Abe Yospe (@Cheeseboy22)

Me: Ok buddy, I know you aren't technically 8 anymore, but we're going to say you are so we can get the kid discount on your ticket.

Kid: Dad, I'm 36.

— Simon Holland (@SimonCHolland)

Me: *holds flashlight under chin* "We're out of wine." Kids scream in terror. Husband arms himself to protect family.

— Linda Doty (@LindaInDisguise)

3yo: Daddy, why are we having chocolate cake for dinner again tonight?

Me: Because Mommy shouldn't go on such long business trips.

— Father With Twins (@FatherWithTwins)

Me: What did I tell you about being bad?!

4yo: Don't leave any witnesses.

I guess she does listen.

— Exploding Unicorn (@XplodingUnicorn)

The way both of my kids argue:

1) Assume you are correct, and that everyone else is stupid.
2) (There's really no #2.)

— Steve Olivas (@SteveOlivas)

My kid walked past her perfectly capable father to ask me for a snack while I was relaxing in the bath. And that, folks, is motherhood.

— Jen Good (@BuriedWithKids)

Ohhh ... I was *so* young.
— 8yo looking at pictures of his 5yo self

— Science of Parenthood (@SciOfParenthood)

Sometimes motherhood is like detention where you have to write out the same sentence 100 times, except you're saying it out loud instead.

— Brenna Jennings (@SuburbanSnaps)

I just want my kids to grow up to be the kind of people who won't camp out in the cold to shop at Walmart.

— Abe Yospe (@Cheeseboy22)

I've mastered the art of opening candy wrappers a few feet away from my kids without them knowing. Skills you can't learn in college.

— Danielle Herzog (@MartinisAndMini)

Before deciding how many kids you want, wrap Christmas presents for that many kids, then reevaluate.

— Linda Doty (@LindaInDisguise)

"Daddy, I want to watch Dora."

"Sweetie, this is Dora. It's the one where she plays an NBA basketball game against the Brooklyn Nets."

— The Walking Dad (@RealDMK)

A parent's lament: "Think of all the sex we could be having if we hadn't had all that sex."

— Kathy Cooperman (@Kathy_Cooperman)

Just to be sure ... when baking cookies for the PTA, do I stick a hot poker in my eye first and then chew glass shards, or vice versa?

— Housewife of Hell (@HousewifeOfHell)

4yo: Why is it called
a piggyback ride?

Me: I don't know.

4yo: Is it because you're fat?

— Exploding Unicorn (@XplodingUnicorn)

Pro Tip: If your son runs into your room at
3 a.m. needing to pee, face him away from
you at all times. At. All. Times.

Sincerely,
Last Night

— Father With Twins (@FatherWithTwins)

4yo: What happens when you die?

Me: You go to heaven.

4yo: No, I mean when you die, do I get your stuff?

— Exploding Unicorn (@XplodingUnicorn)

I wish "There's poop in the bathtub" was just a colorful metaphor.

— David Vienna (@TheDaddyComplex)

> Honey, the kids are
> finally asleep, you know what
> that means we get to do?
>
> Break out the good snacks.
>
> — Simon Holland (@SimonCHolland)

Daughter comes home with shirt inside out.

Me: Why is your shirt on wrong?

Daughter: I think you old people call it "second base."

— So Done Mom (@MomToTeens)

At first it felt weird stirring my cocktail
with this baby spoon,
but if it wasn't for cocktails
this spoon wouldn't even be here.

— Simon Holland (@SimonCHolland)

Sick kid haiku:

2 a.m. wake up
Please aim for my open hands
I have no bucket

— Science of Parenthood (@SciOfParenthood)

Me: What are you up to?

Child: I just put all my dolls to sleep, so you're gonna have to find something quiet to do.

— Paige Kellerman (@PaigeKellerman)

My signature move is spending 4 hours getting my kids to sleep and then tripping over a basket of cymbals on my way out of their room.

— Lurk at Home Mom (@LurkAtHomeMom)

Teenage Girls, if you show up at my door dressed like Miley Cyrus, I'm going to put condoms in your trick-or-treat bags. You've been warned.

— Danielle Herzog (@MartinisAndMini)

My son can now reach the light switches, so don't come over my house unless you're really into raves or want to have a seizure.

— Dad and Buried (@DadAndBuried)

Teen Girl Haiku:

audible eye roll
OMG! FML. *sigh*
text-text-text-text-text

— Housewife of Hell (@HousewifeOfHell)

4yo: Why can't I watch *The Walking Dead*?

Me: Because you're still afraid of the vacuum.

4yo (whispers): Can vacuums be zombies?

— Exploding Unicorn (@XplodingUnicorn)

Aside from the constant threat of the kids falling in or accidentally stabbing me with a molten s'more stick, this fire is totally relaxing.

— Kate Hall (@KateWhineHall)

dry - dry - dry - dry - dry - dry - dry - wet - wet — Me trying to find where my toddler wet the bed in the dark.

— The ParentNormal (@ParentNormal)

My 6yo found the duct tape, and now nothing in my house moves.

— Kalvin MacLeod (@KalvinMacLeod)

My 8yo just came in at 10:45 p.m., whispered, "I have to poop," stared at me for 5 seconds, then went into the bathroom. Parenting at its finest.

— Kate Hall (@KateWhineHall)

4yo: Tell me a scary story!

Me: One time little people popped out of your mom, and they never stopped asking questions.

4yo: Why?

— Exploding Unicorn (@XplodingUnicorn)

Glossary

It's challenging to squeeze comedic brilliance
into Twitter's regulation 140 characters. And
when every letter (and space) counts, you need
some shortcuts. Welcome to the sub-language
of Twitter. You may recognize some of these
mysterious acronyms and abbreviations from
scrolling through your tween's or teen's texts
or research papers. Some are easy enough
to unravel: TY = thank you and YW = you're
welcome. But others are impossible to figure
out. To that end, we offer this handy guide
to Twitter's most commonly used terms and
tweet abbreviations. You're welcome.

AFAIK: As far as I know. In other words, "I have no idea, but I simply MUST chime in."

Avi: The image you choose to represent yourself on Twitter. Everyone starts out as an egg. Don't stay an egg.

Bio: Words you choose to describe yourself on Twitter. Must be 160 characters or less.

DM: Direct Message. Users can send people who follow them direct messages that will not appear in their public stream. Ask permission before sending, some users are vehemently opposed to DMs because they can be spam vehicles, or because they are far too awesome to be communicated with directly.

Favstar: An online service that tracks the most recent and most popular tweets (based on stars/retweets). If you become a paying member, each day you can grant your favorite tweet a virtual trophy. Commonly used by Twitter comedians.

FF: Friend Follower/Follow Friday. Often you'll see #FF followed by one or more Twitter handles to follow. This can be irritating when a person has long strings of #FF tweets and they #FF the same tweeps every week.

FML: F--- my life. Often paired with domestic catastrophes; "3yo just poured herself a glass of milk. All over the couch. FML."

FWIW: For what it's worth. Often paired with IMHO. Synonymous with "I am a know-it-all."

Handle: A person's Twitter username. It's how you're identified on Twitter and always follows an @ symbol. What's your Twitter handle, good buddy?

Hashtag: # is a hashtag. Hashtags are used to group tweets by topic for easy search and discovery. For example, if you searched for "#naptime," it would display every tweet using that hashtag. Hashtags are also used as a "kicker" or the punchline to a joke or statement: #That'sWhatSheSaid, for example. Some people use the word "hashtag" in actual conversation, which is ridiculous.

IDGAF: I don't give a f---. Typically added on to the end of a comment. "I'll take 11 items into that 10-item lane. IDGAF. #rebel"

IMHO: In my humble opinion. Usage of this term is rarely humble.

IRL: In real life. Commonly used for events or meetings that occur in real time with actual, live humans.

LOL: Laughing out loud. Your mom might think LOL means "lots of love." It does not. Do not allow her to put LOL on sympathy cards.

MT: Modified Tweet. Resending an edited version of another's tweet to your followers with proper credit and modification noted. For when the sender just HAS to add their two cents. Many tweeters don't love modified tweets because of their giant egos.

NFW: No f---ing way. As in "There is NFW the 2yo is sleeping in my bed tonight." Spoiler alert: The 2yo is sleeping in your bed tonight.

OH or O/H: Overheard. Example: "O/H from backseat: Boogers aren't gross, boogers are delicious."

RT: Retweet. Retweeting sends an unedited version of another's tweet to your followers with proper credit. Tweeters love retweets because of their giant egos.

Star: Clicking the little star icon is like giving the tweeter a virtual high-five. Many tweeters' entire self-worth is tied up in stars and retweets.

Subtweet: A passive-aggressive tweet directed at another tweep or group of tweeps without mentioning any names. They've been known to cause Twitter Drama. Can also be a nice tweet, but often referred to in a negative manner.

TL: Time line. Where the tweets happen. Shows every tweet by everyone you follow in real time. Eventually, endlessly scrolling through a TL will give rise to carpal tunnel syndrome.

Twitter comedian: All the contributors to this book. Anyone known on Twitter as a joke-tweeter.

TC: Twitter crush. A crush developed on another tweep based on their avi or because they've given your tweets extra attention via stars or retweets. It's kind of pathetic, but happens. It goes something like this: "Why did my TC RT her and not me?"

ToTD: Trophy of the Day. A virtual trophy for Tweet of the Day bestowed upon a particular tweet by a member of Favstar.

Tweep: A tweeter or person who tweets. It's unclear whether this term is cool or nerdy. Or cool because it's nerdy.

QOTD: Quote of the day. The best or most startling line uttered over the course of a day,

"QOTD: Look, Mummy, the baby doesn't even cry when I hit her with this shoe."

YO or yo: Year-old. Used in conjunction with a number to represent a child of that age. For example, "4yo just told me he pooped. In my bed. #KillMeNow"

Contributors

Andy Hardy (@AndyAsAdjective)

I'm wrapped around my daughters' little fingers. Don't tell them I said that. They have HUMONGOUS egos already. My only goal on Twitter is to make myself laugh.

Bethany Thies (@BPMBadassMama)

BadParentingMoments.com

"THAT lady" *eyebrow raised* with the screaming kids is me. Nice to meet you.

Bunmi Laditan (@BunmiLaditan)

TheHonestToddler.com

Wife, mother and writer living in Quebec by

way of California. Creator of @HonestToddler and author of the book *The Honest Toddler: A Child's Guide to Parenting.*

Jen Good (@BuriedWithKids)
The doctor said, "There's two and something else." I said, "Dear God, let it be a tumor." Then I became the proud mom to triplets and their big brother.

Abe Yospe (@Cheeseboy22)
I type words on my home computer and then, using an Internet connection, I post those words to the World Wide Web. In my spare time, I teach first grade.

Stephanie Jankowski (@CrazyExhaustion)
WhenCrazyMeetsExhaustion.com
English teacher by trade, smack talker by nature, Stephanie is a mother of three who lives by the mantra: Life is too short! Laugh!

Mike Julianelle (@DadAndBuried)

DadAndBuried.com

A thirtysomething Brooklynite who is sharing his experiences as a father and bitching about the ways the existence of his son is destroying his social life.

Domestic Goddess (@DomesticGoddss)

UnderachievingDomesticGoddess.blogspot.com

I'm a 50%-er giving 75%! Mom of three boys trying to raise three good men who put the toilet seat down. Professional giggler and philanthropist extraordinaire.

Sarah del Rio (@Est1975Blog)

Established1975.com

Mother of one. Grower of chin hairs. Leaker of pee. One foot in grave. Writer and editor. Writer of the humor blog Est. 1975, for the ladies of Generation X.

Days of Wine and Yoda (@FabLife4)

Tammy Flahive is happily married with two boys. She shares laughs, optimism and tales of burnt toast. Usually found hiding with a cup of coffee (or wine).

Father With Twins (@FatherWithTwins)

I have twin boys and a cool wife. I mostly tweet about things they say and do. My parents stopped following me, so all bets are off.

Chrissy Howe (@FullMetalMommy)

FullMetalMommy.com

Fearless, ever-pregnant mother warrior to three little hand grenades. I share my life like an open book, but keep your grubby mitts off of my chocolate.

Amy Flory (@FunnyIsFamily)

FunnyIsFamily.com

Named one of Mashable's 17 Funny Moms on

Twitter in 2013 and Year's Meanest Mom by her kids in 2014.

Housewife of Hell (@HousewifeOfHell)
Worst housewife ever. Mother to mortified teenage twins. Living a life of minivan madness.

Kalvin MacLeod (@KalvinMacLeod)
I don't know what I'm doing.

Kate Hall (@KateWhineHall)
HallofTweets.com
Stay-at-home mom of three kids. When I'm not answering bizarre questions or wiping poop off the walls, you can find me on Twitter.

Kathy Cooperman (@Kathy_Cooperman)
ReelPlayground.org
Lawyer, mom to four challenging children and writer of upcoming novels about polite mommy crimes.

Kelley Nettles (@KelleysBreakRm)

KelleysBreakRoomBlog.com

I like sloths, Pepto-Bismol, my two sons, my husband, funny people and your new haircut. Writer for NickMom.

Linda Doty (@LindaInDisguise)

JustLinda.com

Momming since '83, Linda's up for parole in 2024 when her fifth and last child turns 20. She hides on Twitter because her kids keep finding her in the liquor store.

Lurk at Home Mom (@LurkAtHomeMom)

You'll see me. I'll be the mom in line for the family bathroom in the mall with tiny ketchup handprints all over my shirt.

Danielle Herzog (@MartinisAndMini)

MartinisAndMinivans.com

Danielle has written for *The Washington*

Post, *Chicago Tribune*, *The Huffington Post*, WhatToExpect.com, Nickelodeon and other national and local sites.

So Done Mom (@MomToTeens)

Stay-at-home mom to four teens. Watch as I fight for my life.

One Funny Mummy (@OneFunnyMummy)

OneFunnyMummy.com

One Funny Mummy writes what she knows: chaos and poop. She lives in Whine Country with her funny hubby, two cheeky monkeys and her dwindling sanity.

Jennifer Lizza (@OutsmartedMommy)

OutsmartedMommy.com

Mom of two energy-filled, lovable boys. Traded in my salary to raise them. They outsmart me daily. It's probably the lack of sleep.

Paige Kellerman (@PaigeKellerman)

PaigeKellerman.com

Writer, humorist and mother. People say I'm a bad cook. They're right. Author of the book *At Least My Belly Hides My Cankles.*

Chris Cate (@ParentNormal)

ParentNormal.com

A three-time parent who prefers to laugh rather than cry during his close encounters of the baby, toddler and kindergarten kind.

The Walking Dad (@RealDMK)

Being a parent is like being a zombie. You're either walking around like the living dead or want to eat their brains. Daddy to twins + one.

Sarcastic Mommy (@SarcasticMommy4)

Trying to be queen of an all-male household with a husband, four boys and a male dog. My life is ... interesting.

Norine Dworkin-McDaniel

and Jessica Ziegler (@SciOfParenthood)

ScienceOfParenthood.com

Two moms searching for answers. Because raising kids defies all reason, logic and most of the laws of the universe.

Simon Holland (@SimonCHolland)

SweetAndWeak.com

If Hollywood made a movie about my life, the actor playing me would be whoever is best at walking around their house turning off lights.

Steve Olivas (@SteveOlivas)

Air drummer in the Twitter garage band; playing gigs when my wife lets me. Please hold your applause until after the kids move out.

David Vienna (@TheDaddyComplex)

TheDaddyComplex.com

Ecstatic I didn't need to pass a background

check to sire my children. My book, *Calm The F*ck Down*, published by @KnockKnock, hits shelves February 2015.

Brenna Jennings (@SuburbanSnapshots)

SuburbanSnapshots.com

Brenna Jennings writes about accidental parenthood at Suburban Snapshots. She lives in coastal New England with her husband, daughter and two ungrateful dogs.

Exploding Unicorn (@XplodingUnicorn)

I'm an upstanding human being, except for when I'm not, which is almost always.

You can read in-depth interviews with many of our contributors at HallOfTweets.com.

Acknowledgments

Our deepest thanks go to each and every one of the Twitter comedians who contributed the funniest, laugh-out-loud parenting tweets we have ever read and whose genuine excitement and enthusiasm for this fledgling project made it SO much fun for us.

Very special thanks goes to Jeff Terry of JeffAndJillWentUpTheHill.com for his valuable help in selecting the tweets for this book as well as for the Top 10 Funniest Tweets lists every month on Hall of Tweets. We've got your pumpkin-spice lattes covered ... for life.

This book would not have been possible without the support of our tireless (and very understanding) husbands. Thanks to Kate's husband, Steve, for putting up with late nights and for doing the heavy lifting with the kids, reading and playing during the editing process. Thanks to Jessica's husband, Greg, for consistently supporting her numerous crazy schemes over the past two decades. And thanks to Norine's husband, Stewart, for patiently building Lego spaceships so she could finish editing this book. (Yes, we can get a babysitter and go out NOW!)

Extra-special thanks go to our kids—Sheehan, Josiah, Autumn, Holden and Fletcher—for just being freaking awesome. Now, come over here so we can cover you in kisses. *Hey! Where are you going??*

Finally, many thanks to all the Twitter

comedians out there who make us laugh every damn day. Never stop.

About the Editors

Kate Hall

If anyone's looking for Kate Hall, check Twitter first. That's where you'll usually find her. She loves Twitter so much that she created a blog, Hall of Tweets, devoted entirely to—you guessed it!—Twitter. Besides her Top 10 Funniest Tweets lists, she conducts "Beyond the Bio" interviews, giving fans a "behind the tweets" peek at their favorite Twitter comedians.

Named one of the 100 Top Twitter Users in Chicago, Kate also routinely makes HuffPost Parent's Funniest Parenting Tweets of the

Week. Her tweets are regularly featured on Modern Mom and NickMom.

When not on Twitter or writing about Twitter, Kate blogs at Can I Get Another Bottle of Whine?, where she writes laugh-out-loud stories about the reality of life. Her essays have also appeared on *Chicago Parent* and *The Huffington Post* and in *The HerStories Project* anthology.

Norine Dworkin-McDaniel & Jessica Ziegler are the co-creators of Science of Parenthood. An illustrated humor blog that uses faux math and snarky science to "explain" baffling parenting situations, Science of Parenthood has been named one of Parenting.com's "blogs every parent should read."

When not pretending to "get" Twitter, Norine

and Jessica are busy writing and illustrating the upcoming book *Science of Parenthood*, based on their blog, which will be released in November 2015.

Learn more about this book, our
contributors, and upcoming volumes
at BigBookOfTweets.com

Be sure to sign up for
special email notifications and
giveaways while you're there!

———————

The Big Book of Parenting Tweets
was created by Science of Parenthood.
Visit ScienceOfParenthood.com to learn more.

16642377R00110

Made in the USA
Middletown, DE
24 November 2018